HOW TO
JUGGLE

25 fantastic juggling tricks and techniques to try!

Nick Huckleberry Beak

ARMADILLO

This edition is published by Armadillo, an imprint of Anness Publishing Ltd,
Blaby Road, Wigston, Leicestershire LE18 4SE; info@anness.com; www.annesspublishing.com

If you like the images in this book and would like to investigate using them for publishing, promotions
or advertising, please visit our website www.practicalpictures.com for more information.

Publisher: Joanna Lorenz
Managing Editor: Caroline Beattie
Project Editors: Sue Grabham and Richard McGinlay
Photographer: John Freeman
Designer: Edward Kinsey
Production Controller: Ben Worley

PUBLISHER'S NOTE
Although the advice and information in this book are believed to be accurate and true at the time
of going to press, neither the authors nor the publisher can accept any legal responsibility or liability
for any errors or omissions that may have been made nor for any inaccuracies nor for any loss,
harm or injury that comes about from following instructions or advice in this book.

Manufacturer: Anness Publishing Ltd, Blaby Road, Wigston, Leicestershire LE18 4SE, England
For Product Tracking go to: www.annesspublishing.com/tracking
Batch: 0233-22319-1127

Introduction

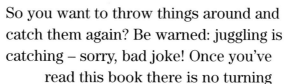

So you want to throw things around and catch them again? Be warned: juggling is catching – sorry, bad joke! Once you've read this book there is no turning back. You'll start with beanbags, then you'll want to juggle fruit and vegetables, next it'll be plates, cups, the furniture, or even the family pet. Before you know it, it'll be double-decker buses or the Statue of Liberty! Nothing is safe. Everything can be juggled.

OK, OK, so I'm getting a little carried away, but that's what juggling is about: fun, trying out new ideas and, most important, enjoying what you do. I'm going to take you through many juggling tricks using bean-bags, coins, rope, cords and, wait for it... cookies and coat hangers! Some of these you will be able to do right away, others will need a little practice, but however you do, I hope that you will find it fun and make it entertaining for others.

Hold on to your hat. Here we go!

Nick Huckleberry Beak

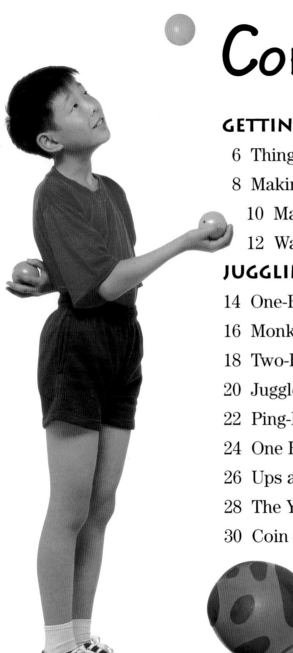

Contents

Things to Juggle

You must have something around the house you could start with right away, like an old tennis ball, an apple or orange, or maybe an old sock filled with rice! Don't try juggling your mother's best dinner plates or your dad's new smartphone just yet. You can, of course, now buy many specially designed juggling accessories, but they aren't absolutely necessary.

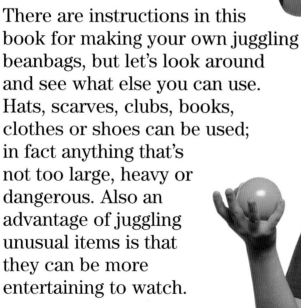

There are instructions in this book for making your own juggling beanbags, but let's look around and see what else you can use. Hats, scarves, clubs, books, clothes or shoes can be used; in fact anything that's not too large, heavy or dangerous. Also an advantage of juggling unusual items is that they can be more entertaining to watch.

However...

It ain't what you juggle, it's the way that you juggle it.

Yes, juggling is fun to watch for a while, but it can get boring, so go on – make it interesting. Tell a joke, wear some bright clothes, make funny noises, and pull a funny face. You'll be surprised how little you have to do to get people laughing and clapping.

Many tricks in this book are fill-ins: quick tricks you can put in between longer tricks so that the audience doesn't know what to expect next. Also, remember even one trick can look more entertaining if you throw the ball higher, lower, wider, faster, slower.

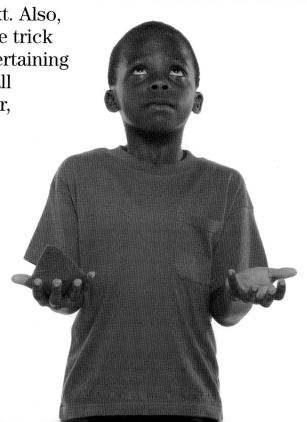

So now you've got no excuse. Get out there and make people happy!

Making Balloon Balls

YOU WILL NEED

Balloons in different shades
Scissors
Small plastic bag
Rice

1 Balloon balls are cheap, easy to make and very eye-catching to juggle. First cut the stems off two of the balloons so that you are left with just the rounded top half of the balloons. Also, fill the plastic bag with a little of the rice.

2 Insert the bag containing the rice into one of the balloon tops. This is a bit tricky, since you have to be careful not to split the bag or the balloon.

TIP

It's worth your while getting good quality balloons since cheaper ones tend to split and often don't stretch as much, which means your juggling balls will end up being too small.

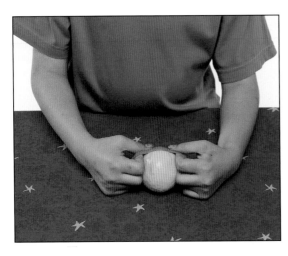

3 Take the second balloon and place it over the ball of rice, making sure it covers the hole left by the first balloon. The hole left by the second balloon doesn't matter, since the first balloon shows through, giving a nice two-tone effect.

4 The next step depends on how fancy you would like your juggling balls to be. Take another balloon and, in addition to cutting the stem off, cut out little pieces from the main part of the balloon.

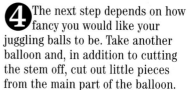

5 When stretched over your ball, these cutout shapes allow the patterns of the balloons underneath to show through. If you like, try a fourth or even a fifth balloon.

Making a Beanbag

YOU WILL NEED

Cardboard, 10cm/4in square
Material
Scissors
Needle
Thread
Small plastic bag
Rice

TIP

Instead of using rice, you can fill your beanbag with dried lentils, millet, corn, or whatever you happen to find in your pantry at home. Each one gives a different feel to the finished beanbag.

1 Using the square piece of cardboard to guide you, cut out two squares of material per beanbag.

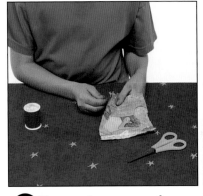

2 Now sew two squares of material together along three sides. Sew the fabric right sides together, since you will turn the beanbag inside out later.

3 Fill the plastic bag with rice. Place it inside the pocket of material you have just made.

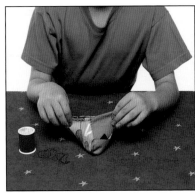

4 Pinch the top edge of your material pocket to form a pyramid. Sew up this top edge and off you go! You are now ready to start juggling.

Warming Up

1 OK, let's start with some simple warm-ups. First place a ball on top of your head. Apart from looking really silly, you are now ready to nod your head and see if you can catch it in your hands.

2 Again, with a ball on your head, tilt your head backward and catch the ball in your hands behind your back. Try to keep your hands away from your back a little since the ball won't roll straight down your back.

3 You've probably seen someone do this one with coins before. Bend your arm at the elbow and put the ball on your elbow. You are going to let the ball roll off and fall toward the floor.

4 As the ball begins to drop, quickly straighten your arm and catch the ball before it hits the floor. Your hand should be facing palm down, as in the picture.

5 If by chance you drop the ball, here are a couple ways of picking it up without bending down. One is to roll the ball with one foot so it rests on top of your other foot. Then flip the ball up to catch it.

6 To look a little more stylish, try holding the ball between the heels of both feet, then jump with both legs up in a backward kick, again throwing the ball up to catch it.

13

One-Ball Workout

1 We are going to start nice and easy, but any of the following tricks can be made more difficult (read the tip). Take a ball, hold it in your right hand and you're ready.

2 Throw the ball just higher than your head and, while the ball is still going up, clap your hands. Keep your eye on the ball.

3 Now catch the ball in your left hand. OK, we know, easy as pie. But try it again, this time clapping your hands three times before you catch the ball.

4 This time, throw the ball up from under one of your legs, still trying to clap before you catch it. A little more tricky, eh?

5 Take the ball behind your back in your right hand, and throw it up over the left shoulder to catch it in front with your left hand. Can you put in a clap as well?

6 The next one really tests your balance and might make you a little dizzy. Throw the ball up with your right hand and spin around.

TIP

To make things a little different, try getting in more claps. You could also try to clap underneath your leg and behind your back before you catch the ball.

7 After spinning round once, catch the ball in your left hand. Feeling dizzy? Can you spin around twice before catching the ball?

Monkey Juggling

No, we are not going to juggle monkeys but turn ourselves into monkeys instead. This is the juggle that everyone can do, but to make it work well you must be a little bit silly.

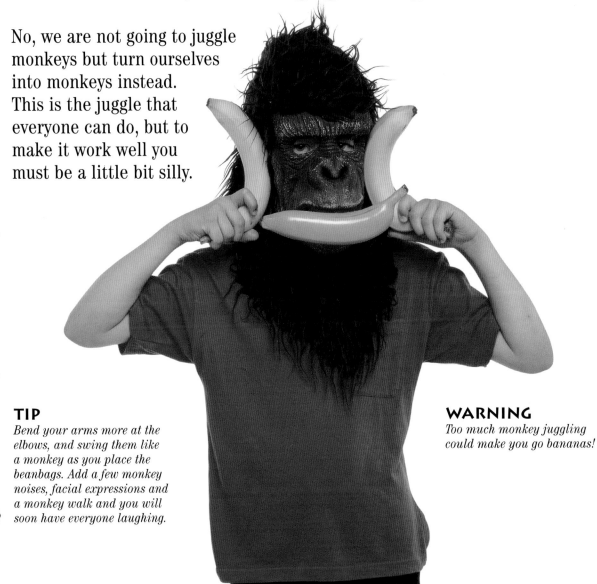

TIP

Bend your arms more at the elbows, and swing them like a monkey as you place the beanbags. Add a few monkey noises, facial expressions and a monkey walk and you will soon have everyone laughing.

WARNING

Too much monkey juggling could make you go bananas!

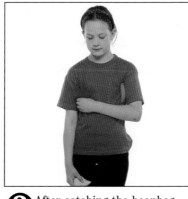

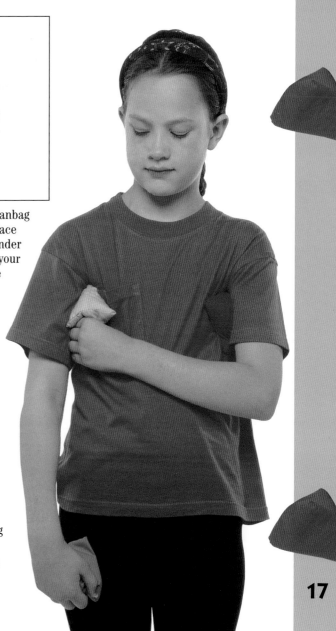

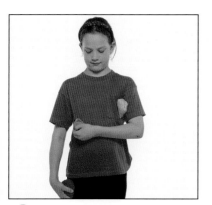

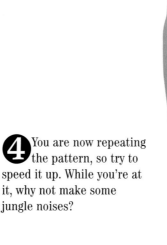

1 Place a beanbag, banana or small coconut under each arm and hold one in your left hand. Cup your right hand, ready to catch the beanbag you are about to release from under your right arm.

2 After catching the beanbag in your right hand, place the one in your left hand under your right arm. Straighten your left arm, ready to catch the beanbag released from under your left arm.

3 Catching the beanbag in the left hand, place the beanbag in your right hand under your left arm and straighten your right arm, ready to catch the dropped beanbag.

4 You are now repeating the pattern, so try to speed it up. While you're at it, why not make some jungle noises?

17

Two-Ball Juggle

1 Don't panic! We're using two balls already, but it's easy. Try it. First, throw both balls up at the same time in straight lines and then catch them. See? Easy.

2 This one looks good, but it's trickier. Throw both balls up at the same time so they cross in midair and land in the opposite hand. Be sure they don't collide!

3 Again, throw both balls up at the same time in straight lines. Before you catch them, cross your hands over. Try not to go cross-eyed!

4 Here we go! If you can do this one, you'll be juggling three balls within 10 minutes. Just relax and try to do this slowly.

5 First, throw the right-hand ball diagonally across, keeping an eye on it. Just as it is about to drop, throw the left ball diagonally the other way.

6 Catch the first ball in your left hand but keep looking at the other ball still in the air.

TIP

*To make these tricks more
difficult, try clapping before
you catch the balls. It's good
practice before you really
start to juggle.*

7 Catch the second ball in
your right hand. Smile –
you've done it!

19

Juggler's Nightmare

This isn't frightening, just difficult to do. It's a good challenge to your friends.

TIP

Show it to others, as even experienced jugglers get fooled by this one. It's not easy, which is why it's called Juggler's Nightmare.

1 This one is difficult, since you will want to uncross your hands when you throw the balls. Pushing your arms against each other will help you overcome this.

20

2 Throw both balls up at the same time so that they cross over and land in the opposite hand. Keep your hands crossed! You'll find you have to throw one ball higher than the other so they don't crash in midair.

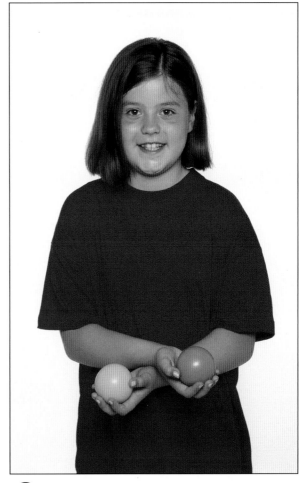

3 Catch both balls. Are your hands still crossed? If so, well done. If not, try again. It can take some time to get the hang of this one.

21

Ping-Pong Nose!

❶ Coat the Ping-Pong ball with non-toxic, clear paper glue and allow it to dry.

❷ Now apply some of the glue to your nose (yuk!) and allow it to dry (it should become clear).

❸ Carefully taking the ball, throw it into the air above your head. Try this a few times with a clean ball beforehand.

❹ Tilt back your head and let the ball drop onto your nose. Pretend that you're clever enough to balance the ball on your nose, and wait for the applause!

TIP

This gets a big response, so really play it up as much as you can. You could replace the Ping-Pong ball with a plastic egg to make it seem more dangerous.

5 Doesn't he look wacky? Your friends will laugh when they see that you've tricked them. Go on, why not make a funny face as well?

One Hand Only

1 Hold two balls in one hand. Side by side is best, but see what feels most comfortable. We're going to start throwing the balls straight up side by side.

2 Throw the first ball up and move your hand to one side to throw up the second one, so that it won't collide with the first one coming down.

TIP

Remember to try this with both hands. Also, you can try moving your free hand around while juggling. Draw a shape in the air or scratch your head with it! It makes things a bit more difficult.

3 Throw the second ball and catch the first. Always keep your eye on the ball in the air. Don't look at your hand when catching.

24

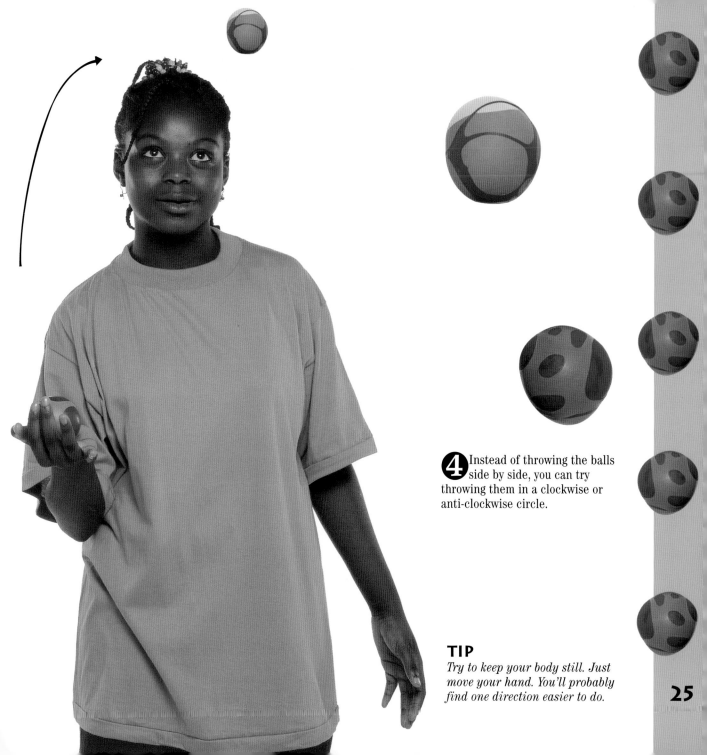

4 Instead of throwing the balls side by side, you can try throwing them in a clockwise or anti-clockwise circle.

TIP

Try to keep your body still. Just move your hand. You'll probably find one direction easier to do.

25

Ups and Downs

1 Now we'll find out if you have perfected the previous trick! Hold three beanbags, two in the right hand, one in the left. Smile – remember you're enjoying yourself!

2 Throw a beanbag straight up from each hand, trying to get them both to the same height. Be ready to throw the third beanbag straight up between them just as they start to come down.

3 After throwing the third beanbag, catch the other two, but still keep your eye on the one in the air. Be ready to throw up the two beanbags just as the third comes down.

26

4 Now you are repeating the trick. Keep it going for as long as possible.

TIP
To make the trick look more impressive, when you throw two beanbags, make them cross over instead of going up and down in straight lines.

27

The Yo-yo Juggle

1 This is as stupid as it sounds, but it looks very funny. Imagine there is a thread joining the two balls together. This means you must try to keep the two the same distance apart from each other when juggling. (Who said this one would be easy?)

2 Raise your upper hand and ball, and at the same time gently throw the lower ball up. You are trying to make it look as if you have pulled the lower ball up with the top one.

3 This time pretend to tie a thread to only one of the balls. Hold your free hand up as if it were holding the thread tight.

4 Lift your upper hand at the same time as throwing the ball you pretended to tie the thread to. Again try to keep the same distance between your hand and the ball.

TIP
Before starting, let the audience see you pretending to tie the balls together with a thin thread. You might even fool some of them!

5 As the "threaded" ball starts to come down, throw up the other ball, leaving a hand free to catch the "threaded" ball.

TIP

With a bit of practice, this looks really convincing. If you really want to impress people, use three balls instead of two. The third ball is held in the upper hand, apparently tied to one of the lower balls.

Coin and Card Capers

1 Carefully balance a playing card on your extended index finger. It's not as difficult as it looks – honest!

2 Holding a coin by its edges, place it on the card directly over the tip of the finger below the card. It's easier if you use a heavy coin, such as a quarter or 10p.

3 Gently grasp one corner of the card, trying to keep your hands steady. This is the moment. Get ready to be brave!

4 Quickly (very quickly) pull the card away, trying not to lift it up or push it down in doing so. With a steady hand and a little luck, the coin will still be sitting happily on your finger.

5 Do you really want to push your luck? Well, set up the coin and card as before, but instead of pulling the card, get ready to flick it with a finger.

6 Ready, set, go! Flick the card quickly and amaze yourself, let alone your friends.

TIP

Be careful to pull the card out horizontally. It is easy to pull it up or down by being too enthusiastic!

31

Three-Ball Frenzy

1 We had to do it sometime, so grab three balls and here we go: your first real juggle. Hold two balls in the hand you throw with.

2 Following the picture, throw the yellow ball up and diagonally across. Get ready to throw the turquoise ball just as the yellow one starts to come down.

3 You've thrown the turquoise and (hopefully) caught the yellow. Be ready to throw the red ball just as the turquoise ball starts to come down.

4 Catch the turquoise ball but keep looking at the red, which you have just thrown up into the air. Yes, it's tempting to look at your hands when catching, but don't do it.

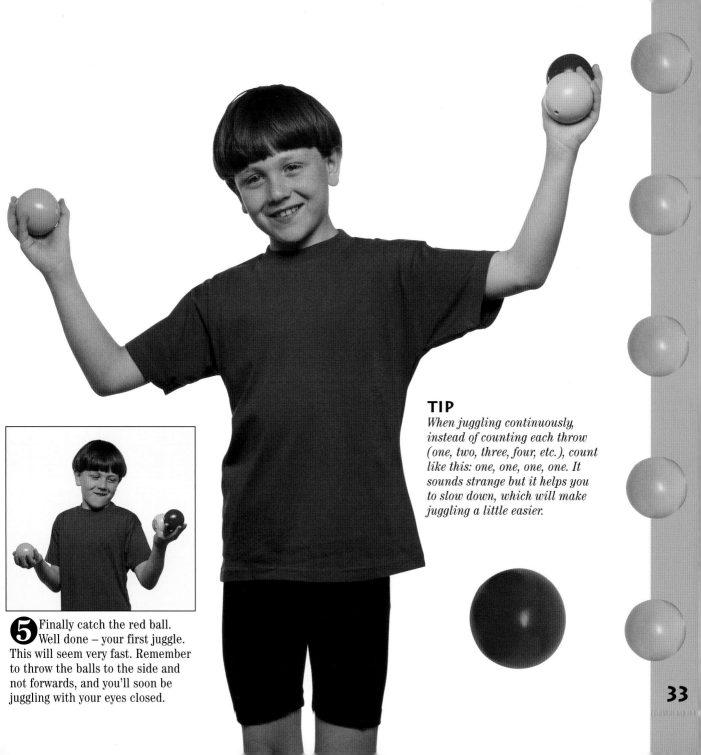

When juggling continuously, instead of counting each throw (one, two, three, four, etc.), count like this: one, one, one, one. It sounds strange but it helps you to slow down, which will make juggling a little easier.

5 Finally catch the red ball. Well done – your first juggle. This will seem very fast. Remember to throw the balls to the side and not forwards, and you'll soon be juggling with your eyes closed.

Flashy Starts

1 Great, you can now juggle. Feels good, doesn't it? Now you have to make it fun to watch. So here's another way to start. Get ready, with two balls in one hand and one in the other.

2 First throw two balls up together in straight lines as we tried out earlier in "Two-Ball Juggle" (page 18). Get ready to throw the third ball just as the first two start coming down.

3 Having caught the two balls, imagine the one in the air is the first ball in the normal juggling sequence and start to juggle normally as it comes down.

4 This is another good flashy start. It always looks very difficult but is really easy. The hand holding the two balls faces down to the floor. Then turn your hand so it is facing up and throw up the balls. Do this quite quickly.

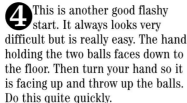

5 See how the balls split to go up side by side as if you had thrown them up with two hands. Try throwing them higher and wider, to see what looks and feels the best. Why not make a funny noise at the same time? It will get a laugh!

TIP
Starting your juggling with different throws always makes it much more entertaining to watch. See if you can invent your own.

Ms or Mr Muscles

This is going to sound and look really stupid, but it is easy to do and can be very funny if done well. It's all up to how well you can act like a fool!

1 Holding three beanbags as though about to juggle, tell your audience you're about to do the Ms (or Mr) Muscles juggle. (Don't worry, you don't need big muscles to do this trick!)

2 Throw one beanbag from your right hand into the air, maybe a little higher than you would normally throw it. You can also throw it straight up above your head rather than to one side.

3 Still looking at the beanbag in the air, bend your right arm and put the beanbag from your left hand right into the elbow joint.

4 Catch the falling beanbag, flex your arm, point with your left hand and pretend you're showing off your enormous biceps (muscles). Really exaggerate your expressions – this is meant to be silly.

TIP
To make it sillier, let the beanbag on your arm drop off but pretend not to notice, so that you are still grinning and pointing but now at nothing. After a little while look shocked to notice that it's gone – the audience will probably have been telling you for some time!

Under or Over

1 Here we go, juggling under our legs! The important thing here is to lift your leg up, rather than bend down to your leg. It certainly makes it easier to balance.

2 Throw the green ball up to your left under your right leg. Keep watching it. Notice that your arm should go right under the leg so that the ball can travel up and not just to the side.

3 Throw the blue ball from your left hand so that you can catch the turquoise one in your left hand. Now you're back to the normal juggling pattern.

4 Finally, catch the blue ball in your right hand. This is really just practice. Now start juggling normally and then throw a ball under your leg and try to keep going – you'll soon get the hang of it.

5 Some more body twisting, this time behind the back. Take your right hand (holding two balls) behind your back and turn your head to look over your left shoulder. Don't stiffen up – try to relax.

6 Now throw the yellow ball from your right hand straight up so that it comes over and above the left shoulder. Your right hand can now go back to its normal position.

7 Throw the turquoise ball from your left hand and catch the yellow ball coming down. Get ready to catch the turquoise ball in your right hand.

8 That wasn't too difficult, was it? As in the last exercise, this is really just practice. Start juggling normally, and then see if you can quickly throw a ball over your shoulder and keep juggling.

Cookie Juggling

It could become a craze! Challenge your friends to try this one and watch the funny faces they make. Not many people can say they have juggled cookies using no hands or feet!

TIP
If you wear glasses, take them off first!

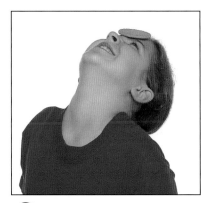

1 Tilt your head back and place a cookie on your forehead. It's best not to use a crumbly cookie, or you will get crumbs in your eyes.

2 Now start making faces and wriggling your facial muscles to try to move the cookie down toward your mouth. Try to keep your head back.

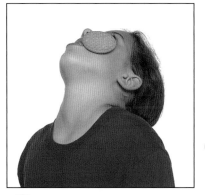

3 Move the cookie down onto one cheek. (Don't move it along your nose or you'll get into real trouble.) You can now tilt your head to one side.

4 With the help of your tongue, pull the cookie into your mouth. You may now bow and take your applause – or you can just eat the cookie!

Body Bouncing

1 These are nice tricks to do in the middle of a juggling routine. Start by throwing one ball in the air, then as it comes down try one of these tricks.

2 Turn your hand palm down and bounce the ball off the back of your hand. Try to bounce it straight up. Sometimes it goes off at funny angles, which makes it harder to catch.

3 Now extend your arm and bounce the ball off your forearm. This one is very easy. You could even catch the ball on your forearm and then throw it up again.

TIP

You don't need to do these one after the other. Just one every now and then makes the juggling more exciting to watch. But of course, if you can do all of these one after the other, you'll get a huge round of applause.

4 Another time bounce the ball off your head (better not to use baseballs!). You can continue juggling after this, but pretend to be dazed and wobble around a little.

5 Just to be really slick, bounce one ball off the side of your foot and continue juggling. Why not invent your own body bounces? You could try it with your knees, shoulders... even your ears!

Juggling Magic

So what's so magical? Well, if you do these tricks with the back of your hand to the audience, they cannot see the ball in your hand. So when you quickly change the balls over it looks as if the ball has changed its appearance in midair. You don't believe it? Well, give it a try.

1 It may not look like magic, but just try it and see. It will take a bit of practice to get right. Close your hand around one ball and rest another on top where your thumb and index finger form a C shape.

2 Now carefully throw both balls up into the air. They shouldn't go very far and should stay very close together, one under the other. Your hand follows them upwards.

3 The same hand snatches the top ball. When you do this quickly, it feels as though your hand simply slides up to take the top ball.

4 Bring this hand (and the ball) down underneath the other ball and catch it on top as before. The above moves are finished before you can say "juggling magic!"

45

The Coat Hanger Swing

1 Go on, show us your muscles! Take a wire coat hanger and with your thumb pull it into a diamond shape as shown. Here we've covered one with red, yellow and white tape to make it look more like a juggling prop.

TIP
No tips for this one.
It's just plain difficult!

2 Hang the coat hanger
upside down from your
index finger and carefully balance
a small coin on the upturned
hook. You may have to bend the
hook a little if it isn't facing up.

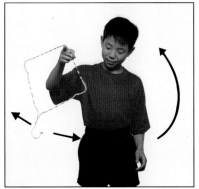

3 Now comes the brave part.
Start to slowly swing the
hanger from side to side. Then
swing it around and around in a full
circle. The coin should stay on the
hanger (but it might fly off, so don't
try this in a greenhouse!).

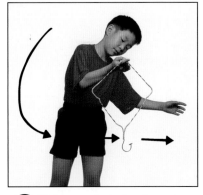

4 Make your last circular swing
a larger one, following through
on a level line. The coat hanger will
now be still and the coin in place.
To prove it's not stuck on, gently tap
the hanger and the coin will fall off.

5 If you're feeling really
adventurous, hang the coin
and hanger from a shoelace and
swing it around as before. This
looks more spectacular, although it
actually seems easier. Anyway, good
luck. You'll need it for this one.

47

Use Your Head

1 Start off with a beanbag on your head (green) and one in each hand (you can use balls, but they tend to roll off your head). Throw the beanbag from your right hand.

2 As soon as the right hand has thrown the beanbag, it reaches up and grabs the one on top of your head (green). Keep looking at the one in the air.

3 Throw the beanbag from the left hand so that you can catch the first beanbag in the same hand. From this point onwards it's just like normal juggling.

4 The right hand throws its beanbag (green) and catches the one coming down. (You've done this before, haven't you?)

5 The left hand throws its beanbag and catches the one coming down (green). Wait for it! The tricky part comes next.

6 As the right hand throws its beanbag to catch another, the left places its beanbag (green) back on your head.

7 Catch the final beanbag in your left hand and – phew – that's it! A long description, but it doesn't take very long. Try to do it again, but start by taking the beanbag with the left hand this time. Go on, it's easy!

Crazy Juggling

1 Having announced that you are going to do an impression of the world's worst baseball team, quickly throw several beanbags into the air as though you are going to juggle them.

2 Open both hands wide and wave your arms about as if you are trying to catch the beanbags, but really just let them all drop.

3 Now that all the balls are on the ground, make a desperate face and pretend to be upset. It sounds strange, but if you act it out well it can look really funny.

TIP
These are extras that you can just slip into your juggling performance to add something different. Don't expect a huge laugh, but they should get a few chuckles.

2 Throw the beanbags in the air as if you are going to start juggling them. It doesn't look as good if you just throw a bunch of beanbags up together all at once.

1 This is how you juggle on a motorcycle: with several beanbags in your hands, hold out your arms to show you are holding the handlebars of a motorcycle Make some engine noises!

3 Then, before they come down, pretend to drive off on your motorcycle. The beanbags should fall down behind you. Keep making those engine noises.

TIP
Put a kazoo in your mouth to make a really good engine noise. You could even wear a helmet if you've got one.

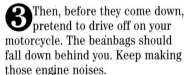

51

What a Mouthful!

1 Start with a ball in your mouth (yellow and orange). That should keep you quiet for a while! You are going to throw the right-hand ball (orange and blue) first.

2 As soon as the right hand is empty, grab the ball from your mouth and return the right hand to a position ready to juggle.

3 Throw the apple from your left hand and catch the first ball (orange and blue) in the same hand. Keep looking at the apple in the air.

TIP
Try this with other fruit, buns, and other food. Be careful when putting things in your mouth. Don't knock out your teeth!

4 Throw the right-hand ball (yellow and orange), catch the apple and start to move your right hand toward your mouth right away. Remember, keep looking at the ball in the air.

5 As your right hand puts the apple in your mouth, your left hand throws its ball (orange and blue) and catches the other one (yellow and orange). Finally the right hand catches the last ball (orange and blue).

Juggling on a String

1 This is a lot of fun and always catches people by surprise. Tie a length of string around a juggling ball. Make sure it's tight since the ball might pop off when you throw it.

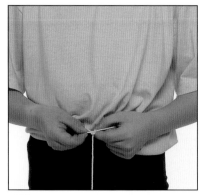

2 Tie the other end of the string around your waist. You could also loop it onto a button on your shirt or jacket; do whatever feels best for you.

3 Now get two other balls and stand ready to juggle. The ball with the string is at the front of the right hand, ready to be thrown first.

4 Throw the ball out in front. It will stop as the string pulls tight. Keep your feet apart to allow the ball to pass back between your legs.

5 The ball will swing up to your back. Sometimes you have to push your hips forward to get the ball to come back up high enough.

6 Catch the ball before it swings down, again. Now try it when juggling two other balls.

7 If the ball doesn't swing well, you may have to adjust the length of the string. It depends on your height, so try different lengths to get the best result.

TIP

Try this trick with a lightweight clear fishing line. This adds to the surprise, since, unless they are very near, people in the audience cannot see the line. Also, you will find you can still juggle normally even with fine string attached, as long as you don't throw the ball too high. So try to start juggling then suddenly throw the ball with the string out toward the audience. You can be sure of getting a response!

Over the Top

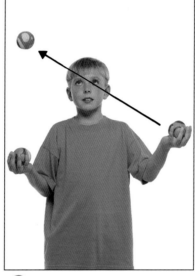

1 Instead of juggling straight across the body, we add a slight change here. Throw the first ball (purple) in an arc over your head. As you can see, you have to swing your arm a bit more to get a better effect.

2 Your left hand then throws its ball (orange) normally across the body and catches the first ball (purple). It will feel strange not throwing the same way from both hands.

3 Again your right hand throws its ball in an arc and catches the ball from the left (orange). If you continue this pattern of juggling it almost looks as if you are juggling in a circle.

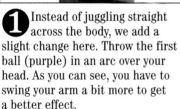

4 Can you guess what comes next? Yes, this time both hands throw their balls over each other in an arc. See how long you can keep this going. Also try throwing the balls higher and lower and see how it changes the pattern and speed of the juggling.

TIP
You can do this throw continuously or just juggle normally and throw an arc every now and then for a change. Remember to rehearse this trick, throwing with the left hand first.

57

Juggling a Knot

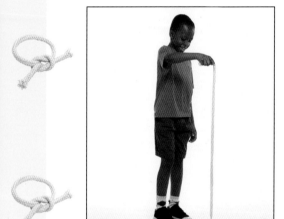

1 This trick is not easy, but please give it a try. You need a length of soft rope (actually, string, clothesline, or anything will do, as long as it's fairly flexible). Ready?

2 Pull up the rope sharply and extend the index finger of the hand that's holding the rope. The rope is now folded over in midair.

3 Hit the rope with your finger sideways and slightly downward. (Don't hit too near the end of the rope.)

4 The rope will swing around and fold over on itself. This all happens very quickly, so you won't see these stages, just the end result.

58

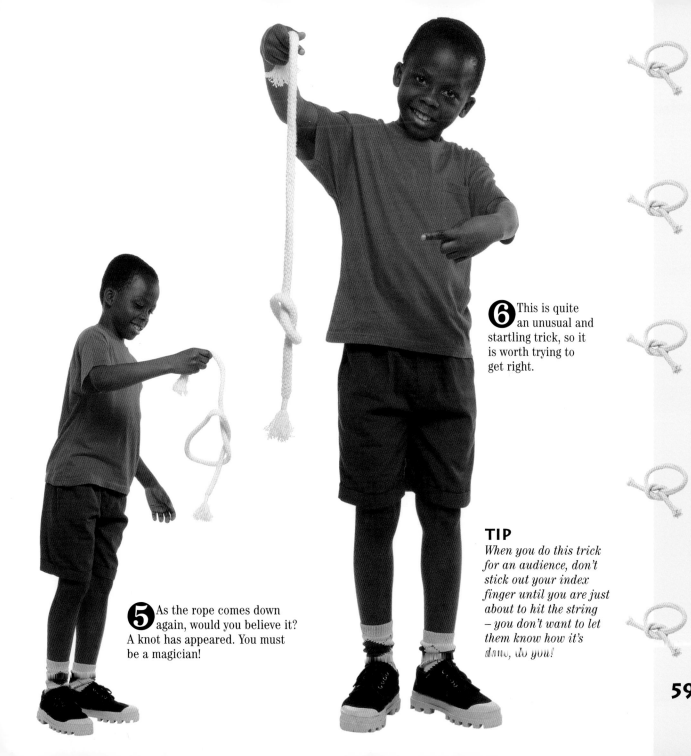

6 This is quite an unusual and startling trick, so it is worth trying to get right.

TIP
When you do this trick for an audience, don't stick out your index finger until you are just about to hit the string – you don't want to let them know how it's done, do you!

5 As the rope comes down again, would you believe it? A knot has appeared. You must be a magician!

Coin, Shirt and Shoe

1 Find a shirt, T-shirt or pullover. To make it slightly easier to juggle tie it in a big, loose knot. This should keep it from flapping around when you throw it.

2 You'll also need a coin and a shoe. Don't use your best shoes, or you'll be in trouble from your parents! The heavier the coin is, the easier it will be to juggle.

3 OK, now you're ready. Let's give it a try. It's probably best to throw the coin first, but you could choose something else. It's not as easy as it looks because of the different weights and shapes of the items being juggled. Time yourself to see how long you can keep going.

4 Why not try other items? So long as it's not too heavy or big, you can juggle almost anything. However, please ask your parents before you try it with a vase or the TV!

TIP

Juggling unusual or oddly shaped items not only looks funny, it makes people think you're a really clever juggler. Juggling food always gets some good laughs, but don't try it with mashed potatoes – what a mess!

Hat-on-Head Finale

1 Choose a hat that fits fairly loosely on your head. It's better if it has a stiff brim as well. (You can tie a scarf round it if you want to.) Hold the back brim of the hat with both hands.

3 Finally, let the hat drop onto your head and spread your arms to signal the applause from the huge audience watching you!

2 Throw the hat up so that it starts to turn over in the air. You'll need to rehearse, as it's easy to over- or underspin the hat.

4 You can also use your hat for your final juggling trick. It just adds that little extra flourish to the end of your routine.

5 Throw the balls you have been juggling up into the air, keeping them quite closely grouped.

7 Turn over your hat and catch the balls in it. Smile – you've just completed a wonderful trick. Remember to take the balls out of the hat before you put it back on your head.

6 Keeping your eye on them, quickly grab your hat with both hands and take it off your head. Don't pull your wig off!

TIP

There are lots of ways to juggle your hat. Try throwing it with one hand, or from your foot onto your head. Think up some different and original challenges.

ACKNOWLEDGEMENTS

The publishers would like to thank the following children (and St John the Baptist C of E School) for appearing in this book: Nichola Barnard, Michael Bewley, Cerys Brunsdon, Alaba Fashina, Fiona Fulton, Camille Kenny-Ryder, Yew Hong Mo, Jessica Moxley, Laurence Ody, Ola Olawe, Tanyel Yusef.

The author would also like to mention the following: Thanks go to Justin from Air Circus and "Smiley Face" from Theatre Crew, Tunbridge Wells, and apologies go to all those who have put up with his practice over the years, especially those in the flat below – thud! thud! Particular thanks (and please keep going!) go to the Bristol Juggling Convention for their enthusiasm.